-Dr. Karen S. Bethea-

Doors Closure CAN BE YOURS

Are You Ready?

Copyright page

Doors

Dr. Karen S. Bethea

Freedombound Publishers
Baltimore, Maryland

Chapter One: The Door Concept

"Hereafter I will not talk much with you: for the prince of this world cometh, and hath nothing in me."

St. John 14:30

There are some seasons in our lives that we must all go through. We will all go through infancy, childhood, puberty, and adulthood. If we live long enough, there are certain seasons like those and others that we cannot get around. We are going to have, as Frankie Beverly sang, "Joy and pain, sunshine and rain." All of us are going to have some good times in life and some bad times. Life is like that. It is made up of good and bad times.

We will have some seasons that we wish we could extend. There are plenty of fond memories that I have of times that I wish I could relive. There are some grown people, right now, who are in denial and walking around dressed like teenagers because they don't realize that season is over for them. Some seasons you can't hold on to. If you keep living, some things that used to stay up by themselves will begin to sag. That is why support garments are big business! There are some seasons that you can't avoid. There will also be seasons that are not so kind and you will not ever want to see them again. I can think of some seasons that I do not care to ever repeat.

These times will come, but that is not the focus of this work. In this book I want to focus on some seasons that I will call avoidable. The reason that the Lord stirred me to write about this is because there are some seasons that we go through that we can actually avoid. There are some seasons that we cause, not the devil, not God, but us. I know it is easier to say, "The devil made me do it" and "The devil was in it" but the truth is that sometimes the devil is not involved at all.

I have found in my own life, and some of you may honestly be able to relate, that there are situations that I have gotten myself into and some seasons that I have caused. I would love to put it on the devil, but the truth of the matter is that it was just me. It was my decision, my disobedience, my error, my mistake, my choice.

Nothing just happens; there is always an explanation for the things that occur in our lives. There is a reason why some men have to keep going downtown to pay child support. It wasn't the devil. There is a reason why some people are broke and their finances are messed up. You can't keep spending the same paycheck over and over and something not come up short. Finances have to be managed and a budget is essential.

Let's talk about "Doors," those areas in our lives of repeated attack and repeated failure. In this book we will learn that some areas we have failed in can be dealt with and closure can be brought to them. We do not have to keep failing at the same old things, unless we just refuse to change.

A door in the natural is a movable structure used to close off an entrance. Doors are necessary because if there is no door on certain things, people that you don't want in certain areas will gain access and end up in there. With locked doors on our homes there are still people that have figured out how to get in. So in the natural, doors are a means of approach or access. You approach a place that is closed off and there is usually a door that will allow you access and entry if you are supposed to be in there. In the spirit realm, a door is a place of vulnerability that allows the enemy to gain access into our lives. It is an area that should be shut, but when the enemy visits our life he finds it open. I believe that the enemy tried all twelve of the disciples when it came time to betray Jesus, but Judas had a door open. He was available and the others were not. There was an area of disloyalty and greed already open in him that allowed him to be used to betray the Savior. While we haven't sold Jesus in the same manner that Judas did, many of us sell Him out every day when we live below what He has provided. He has provided for our victory and some of us are still walking in defeat by choice.

Jesus said in John 14:30, "Hereafter I will not talk much with you: for the prince of this world cometh, and hath nothing in me." What was he saying in this passage? He was explaining the fact that he had no open doors to the enemy.

An explanation is simply a statement that explains or brings clarity. If you walk down the street and see emergency vehicles you will say to somebody, "What happened?" They'll say, "The red car was coming straight and that black car was trying to make a turn. That car ran a STOP sign and they collided." You have just been given an explanation that brings clarity to what you are looking at that you don't understand. An explanation helps you to figure out: What's going on? Why did it happen? What do we have here? It is a statement that reduces complexity. Some of us are always confused. *"Why did this happen to me? Why did this happen to me again? How could this keep happening?"* A curse is a cause of suffering or great distress. Some synonyms for a curse would be misfortune, affliction, trouble, or burdens.

We have two beautiful and powerful texts to help me introduce this concept to you about doors. **Proverbs 26:2, As the bird by wandering, as the swallow by flying, so the curse causeless shall not come.** We just defined curse as trouble, misfortune, and calamity; trouble doesn't just break out in our lives without a cause. Things don't just happen.

When I taught middle school I noticed that a lot of times students had a hard time with connecting the dots and understanding cause and effect. I would walk in the office on my lunch break and somebody would say, "How are you doing Mrs. Bethea?" I would ask, "What are you doing in here?" The student would usually reply, "I don't know." Students don't end up in the office for no reason. I would then ask, "What happened?" Their explanation usually went something like this, "I was sitting in class and somebody...." At that point I would always interrupt them and tell them, "I don't want to know what everybody else did. What did you do that caused the teacher to single you out and ask you to leave the room?" It was amazing how they would always blame someone else.

When I started pastoring I found out that adults don't always understand cause and effect either. They say, "I'm coming to church for help today. Can you pay my rent this month?" They would then get upset when I would ask questions like, "What happened to get you to this point?" They would often respond with statements like, "I don't want you all up in my business." I would think, "Well I'm in there now." If you are asking me to give you eight hundred dollars, I need to know why. If I bail you out this month and you still can't pay it next month, I just wasted eight hundred dollars of the tithes and offerings of our members. I want to know if you ended up here because of a valid reason or because you brought clothes, food or whatever and can't pay your rent." Nothing just happens!

There is a reason why half of your family is not speaking to you. There is a reason why people remarry repeatedly. There is a reason why some people join a new church every year. There is a reason why some people can't keep a job. I met a lady once and she was very intelligent; just plain sharp. She had great educational credentials and an excellent resume. I could not imagine why she was unemployed. As time went on I got to know her and the more she talked, the more I understood why she could not find employment. Her attitude of superiority coupled with a lack of integrity caused her to have trouble everywhere she went. Her skills were great, but she was not. Sometimes people are not willing to put up with great skills if they also have to deal with constant drama. They would rather have peace of mind and work with someone that they have to train. Skills are a head thing, but faithfulness is a heart thing.

There is always a cause and reason for things and it is not always the devil.

In John chapter fourteen Jesus gave a wonderful discourse on the Holy Spirit and explained to the apostles, "I am getting ready to leave you. I have trained you and poured wisdom into you but I am about to go away. Hereafter I will not talk much with you." Jesus understood spiritual warfare. He understood that when you are going through, that's the last time you should be doing a whole lot of talking. When you are going through and in the midst of the battle, the best thing to do is get your favorite song and begin to sing it and minister to the Lord. Why? It will keep your joy level high enough so that the joy of the Lord can be your strength.

When you are going through, the worst thing that you can do is start complaining and bringing a lot of attention to your problem. *"I don't know why I'm going through this. This is terrible. I can't take it. I can't take no more! I'll tell you one thing, I'm about to snap."* Then the devil is saying, "Thank you very much. I must be effective. Let me press you a little harder." Many of us give ourselves away.

Jesus understood spiritual warfare and He said, "I am about to go through the worst hour of temptation that I have ever had since being in this form and on earth with you. I am not going to talk much; I don't have much to say because I understand my assignment. I don't have a lot to say because I am focused. I don't have a lot to say because I need all my energy to make sure I go through with this thing called the cross." The next part of what He said was very interesting. In **John 14:30,** Jesus said, **Hereafter I will not talk much with you: for the prince of this world cometh, and hath nothing in me.** What Jesus was saying was, "I don't have any areas of vulnerability. I don't have any areas where I am open. There are no areas where the devil can attack me and win because I don't have any doors open in my life. Through obeying God, I have shut all of the doors that could possibly be a temptation for me or that could cause the enemy to gain access to my life." He is the only one that can say that. We as human beings have strengths and weaknesses. All of us have some issues and it is nothing that we should feel embarrassed or negative about. We can have issues, but Jesus died to make sure that our issues get resolved. That's the good news! If we are born to humans we have issues.

There ARE doors of access in our lives. Some of us are strong in one place, but there are other places that if you tap that particular spot we will need prayer, oil, and the intercessors! The beautiful part about this is that none of us can judge others, because my door may not be the same one that you have, but I have one. What might tempt me may not tempt you, but we all have doors.

It is those areas of vulnerability that I have identified as doors. When something is vulnerable it is without adequate protection. It is extremely susceptible and open to attack. No one is covering it, no one is guarding it, and there is nothing there to block what is inevitable because it is just wide open like a sitting duck. Those doors in our lives keep some of us going around in circles and failing the same old test repeatedly. Did you ever notice that you are tempted in the same spots all of the time? That's telling you where you are open. Those failures identify our doors. They should give us a clue to what we need to address, conquer, and take into prayer. If we get our eyes off everyone else's faults and begin to look at where we keep getting hit, we will realize that it is an area that is uncovered and that we have not conquered. Nothing just happens, there is always an explanation.

Doors are areas of weakness in our own human flesh and nature that the enemy can take advantage of. He can do it because some of us don't know where our doors are. Some of us honestly and genuinely are not aware of our doors. That would be anyone probably under twelve. If you have been with yourself longer than twelve years, you pretty much know what your doors are. You may not like them, but you should know that they are there. Some of us know that they are there, but we refuse to acknowledge them. Some of us know that they are there, but we feel helpless to change them. Some of us know that they are there, but we don't want to change them because our doors are working for us. The family pays our rent every month because of our doors. You know about that door of sympathy. You know that you should have let Jesus fix that thing, but you won't let Him fix it because everybody feels sorry for you and it is working for you. It causes people to give you money. It causes people to do for you. Whatever the reason, there are doors in all of our lives that need to be shut, monitored, and prayerfully observed lest satan should get an advantage over us.

This principle and concept of doors was introduced to us in **Genesis 4:6-7, And the LORD said unto Cain, Why art thou wroth?** In other words, "What are you mad about? You just murdered somebody so why do you have your lips poked out?" **and why is thy countenance fallen? If thou doest well, shall thou not not be accepted? and if thou doest not well, sin lieth at the door.** In other words, if you open the door temptation is waiting. Nothing just happens!

In this book I want to help those who want to close those doors of vulnerability in their lives. We are never going to be perfect like Jesus, but we can become mature and begin to monitor our doors. Some of us are really good at discerning what others' doors are, but turn a blind eye and a deaf ear to our own doors. Some of us have a critical spirit and are always putting others down so that we can feel better. Some of us are good at picking out the faults in everybody else, but when it is time for God to shed the spotlight on you, you have to go. You are busy and prayer time is over. "I have to get out of here. I have things to do. I am restless because if you make me sit still long enough I will see my doors." This book is for those who are ready to work on themselves!

42 Either how canst thou say to thy brother, Brother, let me pull out the mote that is in thine eye, when thou thyself beholdest not the beam that is in thine own eye? Thou hypocrite, cast out first the beam out of thine own eye, and then shalt thou see clearly to pull out the mote that is in thy brother's eye.

Luke 6:42

Chapter Two: Door Origins

"Neither give place to the devil."
Ephesians 4:27

I want to focus on three areas that can cause us to have open doors in our lives. This is not an exhaustive list, but certainly the most common ones. We can have open doors in our lives due to our lineage, our ignorance, and/or our life experiences.

"Thou shalt have no other gods before me. Thou shalt not make unto thee any graven image, or any likeness of any thing that is in heaven above, or that is in the earth beneath, or that is in the water under the earth: Thou shalt not bow down thyself to them, nor serve them: for I the LORD thy God am a jealous God, visiting the iniquity of the fathers upon the children unto the third and fourth generation of them that hate me; And shewing mercy unto thousands of them that love me, and keep my commandments." **Exodus 20:3-6**

What does this mean? It means that all of us have inherited strengths and weaknesses from our family bloodlines. There are traits, habits, and tendencies that run in our family and are alive and well in each of us. Our ancestors may have done some things that we are completely unaware of but still affect us to this day. Every family has certain traits and everyone in that family has those same traits.

In previous generations, people didn't talk much about family problems. They would slide things under the rug and cover them. You didn't realize until Uncle Chester died that Uncle Chester wasn't grandma's brother but grandma's son that she had before marriage. You didn't know until Uncle Bill died that Uncle Bill had two families. The older folks knew and kept it quiet, but you got to the funeral and noticed that the obituary was longer than it was supposed to be. There were names and faces that you knew nothing about until that day. Issues were never really acknowledged and certainly not addressed. Historically, the focus for many of our ancestors was on survival. They were struggling to make ends meet. This current focus on wholeness and a quality life is relatively new. People are more willing to face things and resolve them in this generation because they want to be happy; they want to be whole.

With all that they did give us, one of the mistakes that our ancestors made was that they didn't tell us some things that we should have known. What happened for many of us as we grew older and reached puberty, was that the "stuff" woke up in us. If we had only known what generally ran in our family, we wouldn't have felt so awkward and out of place when it began to show up. You know that your granddaughter is fast and you say things like, "I don't know what's wrong with that girl." Yes you do! You know first-hand! You know what's wrong because your mama was like that and you were like that. I know that you are saved now, but it was in you. We need to tell our sons that we dealt with anger issues at their age so that their journey to wholeness can be a lot quicker than ours. We have to share out insecurities and struggles as well as our victories.

We have to be honest about what our family is carrying and has dealt with. We can ignore our doors if we want to, but they will work on us subconsciously. They will cut up, show off, act up, and come out when we least expect it. When we don't want them to they will show up. Every family has something.

Have you noticed that in some families none of the women can keep a husband? Have you ever noticed that in some families all of the women in that family are mean? They are pretty and can attract a man but can't keep one. As soon as the brother spends time with them they are like, "No looks in the world are worth all of this drama."

Some families have impatience in their bloodline. Some families have no discipline and everybody in the family is broke. No one ever has money and if one person happens to come into some money, all of them show up at their house to get some of it. There are weaknesses in our family trees that become doors to the enemy, especially when we ignore them, deny them, or won't admit that they are there. Those doors become places of access in us that bring us to places of suffering and great distress. Those doors, when left unattended, become areas through which we suffer misfortune, affliction, trouble, and burdens. Sometimes it is more convenient to blame the devil, other people, or a syndrome for what we refuse to deal with.

Have you noticed that fifteen years ago we didn't have all of these syndromes? All of a sudden there is a syndrome for all these new habits and behaviors. I am not dismissing the validity of some of these problems, but not all of them are syndromes. I cuss you out syndrome. I want to punch you in your face syndrome. Now there is a pill for the things that we won't face. Isn't it amazing that everything that Jesus can wash away and cure suddenly needs medicine? Isn't it ironic that syndrome begins with sin? I have never seen so many syndromes in my life. What it really boils down to in a lot of cases is a lack of self-control. You don't have to curse unless you want to. You have to think those things before they come out. If you think them, you can grab them, and pull them down; you don't have to verbalize them. You don't have to punch the other baby's mother for provoking you. Even that is a choice.

Life is about choices. This stuff is in us, and sometimes we think that once we get saved everything automatically changes. No. The Bible says to work out your salvation with fear and trembling. The blood of Jesus cleanses us and gives us the right vision so that we can now see who God created us to be.

Some of you who were adopted or in foster care should go back and trace your family roots. What happens at puberty is that your family bloodline issues begin to surface. That is why children go through such a critical turning point when they hit puberty. A friend of mine adopted a young boy at age four. When that boy turned twelve he began to exhibit some inappropriate behaviors. I said to her, “You need to go back to the adoption agency and find out what you can about his real parents, because the bloodline that they had is in him.” She said, “I've done everything that I could.” I said, “That is not the point.”

A child's parent can die before that child is born and that child will still grow up with that stuff in him because it's in his bloodline. Many of you parents know that the child in your house that gets on your nerves is the one that is just like you. That is some revelation right there. That is how parents end up with favorites. Some parents like all of the children that don't remind them of themselves. You and your girl clash so much because she is just like you. You and your son clash because he reminds you of you. Our lineage can be a door of vulnerability for us.

Secondly, our ignorance can be a door. Most of the time when we hear the word “ignorant” it is used to demean someone. However, I am not using it in that context. When I talk about ignorance here I am referring to simply not knowing. I mean when someone is not familiar with something or doesn’t understand.

We were in England recently and went to eat. When we came out of the building some guys were over on the field and I said, "What are they doing?" The pastor said, "They are playing cricket." I had never seen cricket played live so I was trying to figure it out. My ignorance about cricket led me to not understand what was going on.

All of us have areas of ignorance in our lives. No one knows everything. There are some things that you are ignorant about. While my ignorance concerning cricket may not hurt me, there are some other areas that you and I can be ignorant about that will hurt us. You can be in a home that is about to be foreclosed upon. There is help available, but your ignorance of that help could cause you to lose your home. In like manner, there is help available to us for our issues and open doors that we simply need to learn about. **Hosea 4:6, My people are destroyed for lack of knowledge.** What we don't know about ourselves can hurt us. This is why we need to pass down stories in families, not just the good ones, but also the struggles. We need to be candid and open with our children and grandchildren. We need to know the bloodline challenges that affect our families. We need to know that kind of stuff. Why? Some things usually skip a generation, but when that thing starts showing up in another generation we need to be able to minister to them and say, "This runs in our family." We need to keep it real with them because it tears up their self-esteem when they feel like they are odd, awkward, and that something is wrong with them.

Some of our family members are messed up with drugs and we need to know that, because if we have an inclination to go that route we can steer clear of it. Some of us have families that are prideful. Some of us are under pressure to live up to a family image that is not real. When a family pretends to be wonderful and perfect what we do is a disadvantage to those coming behind us because they will be knocked off guard and blindsided. We need to let those behind us know things like, "In our family people are short on patience. In our family marriages usually don't last. In our family strife and unforgiveness runs rampant.

Ignorance can leave openings in our defenses that are devastating, and we end up with questions like, "Where did that come from? Why is this happening to me? Why does this keep happening to me? How do I stop this cycle? I thought when I got saved this would end." You are saved, but those doors have to be shut. In my opinion, I don't understand any saved person that is bored. I know that my personal walk with God keeps me very busy and ever reaching forward. I have been saved since I was fifteen, but I know that every time the Lord and I finish dealing with one area of my life, He always finds another one that needs either treatment or improvement. I don't care how anointed I can be in a service, when I get home there is still some flesh that He is trying to pat down. Sometimes it is very frustrating. I asked the Lord one day, "How can you use me so powerfully one minute and I'm so messed up the next?" Doesn't it baffle you at times that God can love you like He does, and use you like He does, even though you really know yourself? When you look at those areas that aren't quite lovely yet you say, "God I don't know how you love me, but I'm glad. Thank you for a second chance. Thank you for not giving up on me because I have some doors that are not so lovely. Behind door #1 is bitterness. Behind door #2 is strife. Behind door #3 is confusion." We all have doors.

Lastly, our experiences can also create open doors in us. This might be the area that troubles us the most, because as we journey through this thing called life there are some situations we encounter that don't leave us the same after we have gone through them. Things that we have encountered in life like divorce, miscarriage, infidelity, betrayal, hurts, wounds, and offences can leave open doors in us. Divorce can leave us with a door of distrust. Rape can leave a door of emotional trauma and turmoil open. Molestation can leave one with a door of fear and shame. Trauma can leave a door open. Crises can leave a door open. Unresolved issues and rejection can leave a door open. Somebody rejecting you as a child can cause you to go through your whole life trying to find somebody that will fill that spot. When you keep trying to find people to make you feel valuable you will soon find that they just don't exist because the only person that can make you feel valuable is you. That is why they call it self-esteem. Self-esteem doesn't come from those around us. It has to come from inside us. Unless we shut that door to self-rejection and fear, we will go through our whole life taking whatever people give us. When that door of rejection is left open we will take anybody that will give us some attention. Why? They make us feel better temporarily. When those doors are left open it makes us vulnerable. Some of you right now can't say no to people who are leeches because you just need to be loved so badly because nobody loved you properly. Anybody that acts like they love you, even if they are just using you, is alright with you because that door is still open. It has made you needy.

You were hurt at one church and you think all pastors are corrupt. That distrust has now become a door that the enemy can manipulate. Every occupation on the planet has good ones and bad ones. There are good dentists and there are bad dentists. There are good attorneys and there are bad attorneys. There are good preachers and there are bad preachers. Don't put all preachers in the same boat.

You can be saved and love God with all of your heart, but still experience defeat, calamity, and drama. You will say, "Why is all of this happening?" **Ephesians 4:27, Neither give place to the devil.** Jesus was the only one that could say He has nothing in him, but you and I have some spots and doors. We have some places that he can still use. Sometimes we become so bitter and unforgiving about some of the things that have happened in our lives that every time we try to go to a new level in God, satan says, "Don't worry about them, I have a door in them. Let them try to go to the next level and all I have to do is latch on. All I have to do is hit that spot. I have a door there."

We have the nerve to blame God. *"I don't know why my prayers aren't getting answered."* When God begins to fill us with what we need to do what we have asked for, we have a door open and there is a draft. The power that we need in order to do what we need to do is leaking out of us. It is not God's fault that we can't hold it. It is that door that He dealt with us about in prayer, that He dealt with us about when the choir was singing, that He dealt with us about during our pastors' last sermon. Somewhere we have been warned.

Do you not know that the devil is not always tempting us, but that at some point we are a temptation to him? There can sometimes be so much open in us that he says, "Ooh! Eeny, meeny, miny, moe; in which door do I go?" He didn't even initiate contact with us. We were so open that we invited him in. *How come my family has so much drama?* It's because of the doors! We can be saved all day long, anointed, and full of the Holy Ghost in our spirit, yet in our mind we are unhealthy because of unresolved issues. Stop trying to make Jesus do what He gave us the power to do. Stop trying to blame the devil for what we won't face up to and let's deal with it.

Places of vulnerability in our lives have to be dealt with in order to close the door to future problems in that area. If we are so diligent about treating a scar that we receive on our body, why are we not as diligent about the scars in our emotions? We can't just keep putting makeup over hurt. MAC is good, but not that good. We can't keep dressing stuff up, *I'm going to just dress up and look good on the outside, but inside I'm torn up!* Eventually there are not enough designer labels to hide your doors or mine. We must address them. Some of our doors require therapy as well as prayer. Doctors treat problems of the body. Psychiatrists treat problems of the mind. Pastors treat problems of the spirit. It all works together. That's why the Apostle Paul prayed for our entire beings in 1 Thessalonians 5:23.

Sometimes our life experiences can leave us with broken doors and broken hearts. Some of us have jammed doors - our doors don't open or close; they're stuck. They are stuck in a season where life has disappointed us. Stuck in a time where things didn't quite work out. Stuck at the memories of a relationship that is over but we aren't ready to turn it loose. Stuck in a place that we never took the time to let the anointing of the Holy Spirit wash over us and heal us. Stuck, jammed, and unable to move!

Some of us have swollen doors. I don't know about you, but when I was a little girl and it rained a lot, my father would say, "Oh Lord, that door is going to be stuck today." Wood tends to expand and constrict. When houses are settling the wood sometimes swells, contracts, and moves. That is how you get some of those little popped nails and cracks. Some of us have had so much rain in our life, so many trials, so many tribulations, so many tests, so many disappointments, and so many heartbreaks that now our door is swollen and can't fit back in the door frame because it is full. It is full of residue. It is full of baggage. It is full of bad memories. It is swollen.

Some of us have doors that have come off the hinges. We have been through so much that our doors are hanging by a thread. Some of our nails have fallen out. There has been so much wear and tear on our lives that our doors are half on and half off. The danger here is that a hanging door is not fulfilling its proper function, because you can't close it? Something has been left unprotected by a door that is malfunctioning.

Some of us have cracked doors. Some of us have made some poor life choices and those choices have caused our doors to become damaged. They are damaged to the point that we can't put sealant on them and fix them up. There are holes where holes shouldn't be. He walked off and left you and took half of your heart with him. Instead of your whole heart belonging to Jesus you gave it to flesh and flesh broke it. Flesh did what flesh does. Some of our doors are so messed up that we need a door replacement. Take this door and give me a new one because this one is so messed up, so cracked, so bent, and so scarred. Don't paint over my stuff. Give me a whole new door! David said, “Create in me a clean heart and renew a right spirit in me.” This heart has been through too much and it will not function in my future. It has too many holes, too many cracks and missing elements. God just give me a new heart.

Some experiences will leave us with doors that no longer have the capability to guard our heart like they are supposed to. They no longer have the capability to open at the right time and let the right things in and shut at the right time and keep the wrong things out. The door just needs to be replaced. The good news in all of this is Jesus is the ultimate door fixer!

Chapter Three: Gideon's Doors: A Biblical Example

Unresolved issues can cause us to abort the will of God for our life. This was almost the situation with Gideon in Judges 6. You may be able to relate to Gideon. Some of us will be able to relate to it because it is our past. Some of us will be able to relate to it because we are there now. Some of us haven't lived long enough to get to this point, but when we get there we will have a word in advance of it so that it will help us navigate through life's seasons.

One thing that I love about the Bible is that God never hid the flaws of the major characters of His word. He let us see people for exactly who they were. In the word of God we have some positive examples of what to be, but we also have some negative examples of what not to be. There will be people in our life who are a wonderful example of what to be and to do. We will also have examples of what not to be and what to steer clear of.

In **Judges 6** we find the children of Israel under the oppression of the Midianites and Amalekites. They had fled to the mountains and started living in caves. When we are disobedient to God, we will end up doing some things that we said we would never do. We really can't go through life talking about what we won't do because if the right set of circumstances hit our life we will or we will think about doing things that we never thought we would. God had created them for greatness and they were living in caves! In the pattern of the Old Testament, God would bless the children of Israel and things would go well for them. However, as soon as things started going really well they would forget who blessed them, forget who brought them out, and fail to heed the Lord's warnings. God would always bring them out and say, "Don't serve strange gods. Remember that it was me, the Lord your God, that brought you out of Egypt." They would say, "Yes, Lord." When we want what God has we are very agreeable. *"Yes, Lord. I promise. God you have me forever, if you bring me out of this!"*

As soon as things were going well they did exactly what God asked them not to do, they disobeyed Him. Every time you disobey you enter into a cycle of disobedience. Disobedience breeds disorder, and disorder breeds drama. So they were back in that same cycle and became captives. God created them to be conquerors, but they were captives. Like some of us, God did not create us to live like we are living. We are living the life of a captive when God said, "I came to set you free and make you more than a conqueror. I am going to do exceeding abundantly above all that you can even think or ask for."

The children of Israel again were brought low. Whenever we depart from God we are going to live a low life. It might start off looking okay, but eventually things will go downhill. The children of Israel cried out to the Lord in their desperation. Whenever they cried out to God, He would raise up a deliverer. In Egypt they cried, "We want to be free," and God raised up Moses.

God raised up a deliverer for them. He first sent the prophet to remind them of their rebellion and idolatry. What I love about the Lord is that we can be as messed up as ever, but if we really cry out to Him with a genuine heart God will meet us right where we are and take us to where we need to be. The wonderful thing about God's love is that He doesn't come condemning and judging. He doesn't throw our faults in our face. He doesn't have a whole hour long dialog to decide if He is going to deliver us. **Come now, and let us reason together, saith the LORD: though your sins be as scarlet, they shall be as white as snow; though they be red like**

crimson, they shall be as wool. (Isaiah 1:18) What that means is, "I will take the residue of the situation. I will remove it to the point that no one will ever believe that was you."

They cried out unto the Lord and the angel of the Lord appeared unto Gideon and said unto him, "**The LORD *is* with thee, thou mighty man of valour.**" Gideon was nobody's mighty man of valor. Gideon was timid, nervous, and didn't have any confidence. Isn't it beautiful that when God deals with us He doesn't look at us in our current state, but begins to speak to us according to what He created us to be? God walks up to him and says, "You are a mighty man of valour." Don't you like the fact that when God deals with our life He has a future focus? He is not picking apart where we are presently and He is not judging us for our past, but coming and letting us know what the potential is for our life. He is speaking into our future and letting us know what He created us to be if we would dare pay the price to be that.

He called Gideon a mighty man of valour. Gideon was shocked! **And Gideon said unto him, Oh my Lord, if the LORD be with us, why then is all this befallen us? and where *be* all his miracles which our fathers told us of, saying, Did not the LORD bring us up from Egypt?** What is happening here is

Gideon is a second generation Israelite. He wasn't alive when God parted the Red Sea and he did not see all of the miracles. That is why it is so important for us to pass down our heritage and culture to our children. We must help them understand that we didn't always act like we do now. We must pass down the things that grandma did like, "Don't leave the house before you get on your knees. Before you go to bed at night ask God to forgive you for anything that you did that day. Before you lay down at night forgive anybody that offended you." We have to be careful to pass down the good things in our culture.

Gideon was not connecting the dots, because the first thing that he wanted to talk to the Lord about was, "How come we are in bondage?" In **Deuteronomy 28,** God said, "If you obey me you can count on all of these blessings to come on you and overtake you." In verse sixteen He goes on to say, "If you don't do like I have asked you, you can expect all of this to come on you and overtake you." Some of us take the sovereign thing out of context by saying, "God can do anything, how come He doesn't just do it?" God won't break the rules that He has set up. God said, "I gave the earth to you Adam to guard, dress, and keep it, but instead of taking good care of the earth, through greed, you have cut down everything, torn up everything to make more money, and now we have pollution, crime, and cancer. If you had done things the way I asked you to, you wouldn't be experiencing some of the problems that you now have. However, even though you have messed up I am still a holy God. If you ask for my help I will come down and fix it. I can't just come down and take over, because I gave you dominion. Therefore, there are boundaries to my intervention. If you want me to intervene you have to ask me." Prayer is the vehicle that brings divinity into the affairs of humanity. God told us, "You have not because you ask not." *"Where is God at?"* I can hear Him saying, "Where is the prayer? I searched the earth and I couldn't find anybody standing in the gap. If I could just find somebody to get in agreement with me I can fix things. Will somebody pray?"

When God wanted to bring Jesus into the earth He couldn't just throw Him down here. He had to find a vessel. He had to find somebody that would get into agreement with His will. That is all God needs from us. Faith is agreeing with what God said. God is always looking and He said, "I looked and wandered; there was no intercessor." Faith is when we get in agreement with what God can do and wants to do. When we live our life and don't pray, we have not because we ask not. Where is God? Waiting on us!

God goes to Gideon, and because of the cry of the children of Israel God said, "I am going to raise up a deliverer." God will go to somebody like Gideon. God comes down to Gideon **and the LORD looked upon him, and said, Go in this thy might, and thou shalt save Israel from the hand of the Midianites have not I sent thee?** Because of his doors, Gideon was not able to believe what God said about him and his wonderful future! In other words, the Lord was saying, "Listen child, do you understand I am talking to you? I am not your aunt Mable, I'm God. I am the creator of the heavens and the earth. I am Alpha and Omega. I am the one that parted the Red Sea that you heard about. Do you not understand?

And he said unto him, Oh my Lord, wherewith shall I save Israel? behold, my family *is* poor in Manasseh, and I *am* the least in my father's house. Isn't it amazing that when God begins to speak to us and tries to give us a future, many of us cling to our past? God just called him a mighty man of valor and all he wants to talk about is the fact that he grew up poor? When did that enter the conversation? God said, "I created you and you are a mighty man of valour. You are having an identity crisis right now because you think your problems are who you are. Your problems are problems, but they don't define you."

Some of us have become so closely knitted with our doors that we have an identity crisis because we don't realize that we are more than a conqueror and not a captive. The problem was never meant to take us out, but to build us, strengthen us, and encourage us. It was meant to give us something to overcome so that we could get more power in our life. It was only a temporal situation. That wasn't the end, but a season that we were supposed to pass through, to build us, strengthen us, and make us able to relate to the people that God was going to use us to help. Sometimes what we go through is not just for us but for the people that God is going to use us to minister to. How can we help them if we've never been there?

God is trying to take this boy into his destiny, but the door of shame, pride, and low self-esteem is keeping him from what God has for him. The devil was not in the conversation. The devil was not even there. Sometimes our life experiences can be so bad that even God can't get us to come out of there. God said, "Gideon, you all are torn up. You all are in captivity. Everybody is bound and things are a mess. You, mighty man of valour will bring them out of bondage." God said, "I knew where you were from when I called you. I know about your past, that's why I picked you. There are a whole lot more people just like you and I am picking you because you will be able to set them free. Once I get you free you will know the symptoms, how to smell it, how to pray for it, and then tell them how to come out and stay out."

Some of us are ashamed of what God is trying to do in us because we don't understand that our past is not something to be ashamed of, but rather it is something to celebrate. We can't celebrate it when we are still in it. We don't want to talk about it when we are still in it. How do we know when we have come out of it for real? We know when we can tell it without being ashamed. We can tell it without getting an attitude. I don't care about who knows about my ex-life because it is my ex-life.

Gideon can't receive from God because of an open door in his life. The thing that was holding Gideon bound didn't just happen. The thing that is preventing us from walking in the will of God right now for our life didn't just happen, the devil started early. If we are honest, most of us today are struggling with stuff from childhood. I know you didn't think all that was spiritual. We became a member of a church, learned how to act religious, but didn't let God get on the inside. When we are free, we don't have to act. I don't have to act religious. I don't have to act spiritual, I am spiritual. It comes out of everything that I do.

Gideon was struggling with the fact that somebody like him, born in a family like his, poor and impoverished couldn't be used by God. Some of you have been in church too long to still look like you look. Some of us have been in bible study, had hands laid on us, been to revivals, conferences, meetings, and intercessory prayer circles and still won't let God do what He is trying to do in our life. It is not the devil, our neighbor, or our spouse, but simply those doors that have not been addressed, those doors that are jammed, those doors that are cracked, those doors that are swollen, and those doors that are off the hinges that are not allowing the spoken word of God to manifest in our life.

God puts the desires in our heart and then comes and says, "I'll give you the desires of your heart." All he needs is for us to get in agreement. I am a living witness. God will put the desires in our heart if we get in agreement with Him and His desires. That is why, if we ask anything according to His will, He does it.

Some of us can't get encouraged because we are holding on to the past like Gideon. *"I came from a poor family. I don't have nothing. Nobody in my family ever did anything significant."* As long as we look back and hold on to that, we can't see what is up ahead. How do we know when we believe God? We will start speaking it. You will start to speak what you hear Him speak.

Sometimes we have to have a paradigm shift in order to do God's will. A paradigm shift simply stated is a change of mentality. I didn't believe in women pastors. God had to change my viewpoint in order for me to walk in His will. Some of you today are struggling in your mentality with some things that you think, believe, and have held dear. They aren't things out of the Word, but stuff that your grandma or someone you respect may have said and you are struggling to let it go.

God had to change Gideon's mentality so that he didn't abort what God had for him. He had to take him from seeing himself as a victim to a victor. Many of us are so married to our situation of the past that it is crushing, destroying, and killing any chance of us walking in what God has for us and the devil is nowhere on the block. Don't let anyone steal what God has put in you. If God said it, He will do it and bring it to pass.

Close the door. Let's shut it down and get it out of our way. God has great things for us. **Eye hath not seen, nor ear heard** the things that God has in store for us. Let's shut the door on our excuses. If God called us, He knew what we were before He called us and He is more than able to fix whatever needs to be done in us. **Colossians 2:10, And ye are complete in him, which is the head of all principality and power.**

Chapter Four: Guarding Doors

"Keep thy heart with all diligence; for out of it are the issues of life. Put away from thee a froward mouth, and perverse lips put far from thee. Let thine eyes look right on, and let thine eyelids look straight before thee. Ponder the path of thy feet, and let all thy ways be established. Turn not to the right hand nor to the left: remove thy foot from evil."

Proverbs 4:23-27

"Then answered Peter and said unto him, Declare unto us this parable. And Jesus said, Are ye also yet without understanding? Do not ye yet understand, that whatsoever entereth in at the mouth goeth into the belly, and is cast out into the draught? But those things which proceed out of the mouth come forth from the heart; and they defile the man. For out of the heart proceed evil thoughts, murders, adulteries, fornications, thefts, false witness, blasphemies: These are the things which defile a man: but to eat with unwashen hands defileth not a man. "

Matthew 15:15-20

God really wants to close up some spots in us, because there are beautiful people who genuinely love Him, but are suffering silently because of their doors. We can genuinely love God but still have some doors open. Some people have said, "How come I haven't grown any further? It looks like I keep reaching out." When there is a draft, what we take in doesn't stay. Instead it seeps out because we have doors open. The power that we need to grow keeps slipping out of us because there are some doors that need to be shut. When you have the air conditioning on at the house you say, "Shut the windows and doors." Why? "I need the air to stay in here." God needs His anointing to stay in our life, but it can't stay in there when we have doors open - doors of rejection, doors of fear, doors of insecurity, doors of poor self-esteem, and doors of lack. Those doors are stripping us of the power that we need to be victorious.

Once we recognize our doors we must then begin to guard them. It's not the type of guarding that denies what our doors are, but instead we recognize what they are, deal with them, and know that they are places of vulnerability that we have to keep our eyes on. We can be saved but we still have to work out our salvation with fear and trembling. (Ephesians 2:12) Our flesh will never be saved because it has imperfections, it has challenges, and it is not subject to the law of God.

For this reason, the door to our hearts must be guarded. We must protect it, cover it, and make it secure. Our heart, in the natural, is the chambered muscular organ that pumps blood received from the veins into the arteries, thereby maintaining the flow of blood through the entire circulatory system. Our heart pumps blood throughout our entire body. Whatever is in our heart in the natural gets pumped out and goes into our whole body. That affects every part of us. By the same token in the spiritual realm, whatever is in our heart affects our whole entire being. It affects how we see, what we believe, what we say, our emotions, and our mentality. If the heart is not right then everything else is off, because what is being pumped out of our heart to our whole being will be off. We must shut our doors because they affect everything. Proverbs 4:23 is clear that our issues come out of our hearts. Jesus made it clear that what goes into us is not what defiles us, but what comes from the heart.

The heart in the spiritual realm is the vital center and source of one's being, emotions, and sensibilities. It is the repository of one's deepest and sincerest feelings and beliefs. It is the seat of the intellect or imagination. Everything about us in the natural, whether healthy or not healthy, whether we have a high energy level or low, whether we are anemic or have a rich blood flow, depends on our heart's ability to pump blood properly to every area of our body. What we are in the spirit realm has everything to do with what is coming out of our heart and whether our heart is right.

People amaze me sometimes when they curse and turn around and look at you and say, "Excuse me." I always say, "God heard you. You need to tell Him that you are sorry." The real problem for me is not that they cursed, but that it was in their heart to come out of their mouths." We spend a whole lot of time trying to fix our words but our words come from our heart. If we focus on our heart, we won't have to worry about our words. We often think we need to watch what we say. The truth is we need to watch what is in our hearts. Whatever is in our hearts eventually will come out. There is going to come a moment where we are not as guarded as we normally are and it is going to seep out anyway. Why, because it is in there. If our heart is right, our words will always follow. We spend an abnormal amount of time trying to impress people, by saying the right thing, and doing the right thing. Just be right.

We must guard what we hear, think, and allow to enter into our hearts. It is better to shun the bait than to struggle on the hook.

We must guard what we hear. **Keep thy heart with all diligence; for out of it are the issues of life.** Most people quote verse 23 but skip the rest of it. P**ut away from thee a froward mouth, and perverse lips put far from thee.** The perverse lips and froward mouth come from when the heart is not guarded. They come from the things that have crept in. **Let thine eyes look right on, and let thine eyelids look straight before thee.** When our heart is off our focus is on the wrong things. Our heart is messed up and so is our focus. An inappropriate focus brings inappropriate words. When we are not looking right and our perception is messed up, than our words begin to get messed up too. It's all related.

Ponder the path of thy feet, and let all thy ways be established. When we are not looking right we are not walking right. When I walk I am usually walking in the direction that I am looking. Most people don't walk looking another way or backwards. When our focus is off because our heart is off, our hearing and eyes are off, and so we end up bumping into stuff that we shouldn't or normally wouldn't. We end up being taken off guard because our vision is off and we are not able to see what we ought to see. Sometimes we see what is not because what we believe is off and so what we see is off.

The amplified version says, **Keep and guard your heart with all vigilance and above all that you guard, for out of it comes the springs of life**, the issues of life. All of our issues start in our heart. The reason why you don't like other women starts in your heart. One sister took your man and now you don't like any of us. That's a door that the enemy can now tap into. God can send somebody to be a prayer partner and a real friend to you, but you can't receive her because the issue of your heart says, "Don't trust women." That is now a door that the enemy can play with. Every time God sends somebody into your life as an answer to your prayer she can't get in, she can't reach you, she can't make the deposit that God sent her to bring to you because of that door.

One bad experience with a doctor and now you think that all doctors are corrupt. Yes, there are some corrupt ones, but there are also some wonderful ones. There are some that are full of integrity, treat people right, and take good care of them. You have to keep searching and ask God to lead you to a good one.

The heart should be guarded for out of it comes one's actions. Here, the word "heart" means more than mental or emotional capacity. It encompasses one's values. These verses apply the command to guard one's heart including what one says, sees. and does. The mention of the mouth and lips is similar to Christ's teachings on the relationship between one's heart and his speech. If you want to know what somebody really feels, get her mad. When we get mad as humans, we usually say what we really feel. What we say when we are mad is really what we mean. When we are mad we don't have time to think, be appropriate, fix it up. or act spiritual. We are mad and it comes up and out; pure, uncut, and unedited.

We must guard what we hear. The Bible says to give no place to the devil. **(Ephesians 4:27) Proverbs 18:21, Death and life *are* in the power of the tongue: and they that love it shall eat the fruit thereof.** We can either speak life or death out of our mouth. I did an experiment years ago because when I got saved I was very negative. If nothing was wrong I would find something to worry about. I would fool around until I had a problem. I was so used to things not working out that I was uncomfortable unless I had a problem. If the day was going well I would start saying things like, "Something is about to happen, I just know it. Everything is going too well. Things are going well so something is going to happen real soon." I would keep talking like that and I wasn't happy until I said, "See? I told you. I knew something was going to happen, I felt it." I was saved, loved God, spoke in tongues, but was full of fear. I began to pay close attention to my words all day long and I found that my words were a door that kept my faith from functioning properly. My negative confessions and comments were killing my prayers.

I remember when I was a little girl and I had that doll Dancerina. I got Dancerina for Christmas and I said to my brother, "She is going to break," and the doll broke. I realized the power of life and death was operating even then. I said, "See? Everything I get breaks on me." Every Christmas one of my toys would break. My father would say, "The stores are all closed today so we can't take it back." I would say, "That's alright. That's how things work out for me. I knew something was going to break, probably the thing that I wanted to play with the most is going to break." I was so negative. I wasn't happy until something was wrong. Something would happen and I would look for the bad in it. If something good would happen, I would say, "I'm going to keep going because something is wrong. This is not perfect. Something is wrong here and I am going to find it." The Lord began to show me, "You believe what you say." People could encourage me and I wouldn't believe them because what I had said to myself was what I believed. We are forming our future right now by our mouth. The life that we are living today has been shaped by our words.

This principle can work on the positive side as well. I am so glad that everyone reading this book hasn't been speaking negatively. Many of us have been eating the fruit of our lips, and it is good stuff. We have been walking according to **Deuteronomy chapter 28,** and the blessings of the Lord have been overtaking us because we have been setting ourselves in agreement with the Word. We have to subject what we think, say, and feel to the Word of God.

The ear is one of the doors to our spirit. What gets in our ear is important because what gets in doesn't just go in there and sit; it has an effect on us. Some of us had people speak negative things over us as a child and to this day we have had to fight just to feel good about ourselves. We weren't our parents' favorite, so we suffered. Some of us had negative parents and people spoke things like, "You're just like your mother or you're just like your daddy." It may not have been a positive comparison. We heard those kinds of things growing up and it has taken us our whole adult life with the grace of God and power of the Holy Ghost to get that stuff out of us. What went in our ear got in our heart and our heart believed it and you acted on it. We have to guard what we hear. The wrong things in our ears can cause doors to develop in our lives.

The words of a talebearer *are* as wounds, and they go down into the innermost parts of the belly. Proverbs 18:8

Talebearer is a nice and neat way of saying a gossiper. One of the things that we have to guard our ear from is gossip. There are people at our church who know the rumors around our church better than they know my messages. They have an appetite for mess. You can say all day long, "People just feel like they can talk to me." But the truth is they know that you are a human trashcan. Whatever junk is going around the building you will be more than happy to hear it and suck it up. People don't come to me with gossip because I don't have an appetite for it. I don't have a taste for it. I don't have a desire for it. People know when they can talk mess to you. People know when they can come to you. If they comfortable coming to you it is not a compliment, because it means that like spirits have connected. They are not about much and they know that you aren't either. They know that you don't have a prayer life and they don't either. We know who to go to with our mess don't we? It is not a compliment when people call us with junk and garbage.

The words of a talebearer or gossiper go down into our spirit and lodge there. We can tell when someone has been talking about us. The next time we encounter her, things are different. She will look all around and can't even give us eye contact. Someone has infiltrated her ear and it has affected her interaction.

Those words go down into us and lodge there. They become wounds and now our spirit is wounded and we are not the same. That thing has taken root. That is why the Bible says to tear down strongholds and cast down imaginations. At the point that we hear something we have to snatch it down. If we don't snatch it down and it takes root we are going to bear fruit from that thing. We are about to see a manifestation because we have seeds and seeds grow. Let's say that somebody comes to me and plants something into my spirit about someone. The next time I see her my interaction is going to change. She may not even know what changed but she can feel when something is different. A door is now open.

I can tell when somebody is getting ready to make a negative deposit and God has shown me how to lovingly shut her off. If I never hear it I don't have to fight it out of me. It is easier to shut the door than to clean it out, it's proactive. It is easier to have never heard the mess than to get the mess out. With the destiny that is over our life, we need all of our energy to birth what God has put down on the inside of us. We don't need to waste energy fighting over gossip and foolishness. We need all of our energy and the doors shut so that we can keep everything in that is fermenting the will of God down on the inside of us. We don't need any junk, garbage, and confusion that we have to fight out because every moment that we spend on mess we are missing an appointment with God, missing an appointment with destiny, and missing time that we could be working on what God has called us to be. Every moment that we waste on junk, we are missing out on becoming the real us.

Some people want a perfect church full of perfect people, but that is never going to happen. Everything in a church house is under construction. Because Jesus shed His blood for all of us we have the right to come as we are and get delivered. We have a right to come with whatever doors exist in us and get answers and healing.

As a pastor, I would rather for somebody in our house to be a weak saint than become a strong sinner. I would rather for them to stay in the house and keep crying out to God, praying, getting the word, and working on their doors than just being turned away altogether and we lose a member from the body. (Hebrews 12:12-14) We are connected and need one another.

We must guard what we hear, what we think, and what we let enter our hearts.

Chapter Five:
Door Repairs

KJV

"Therefore if any man be in Christ, he is a new creature: old things are passed away; behold, all things are become new."

2 Corinthians 5:17

Amplified Bible (AMP)

17"Therefore if any person is [ingrafted] in Christ (the Messiah) he is a new creation (a new creature altogether); the old [previous moral and spiritual condition] has passed away. Behold, the fresh and new has come!"

The Message Bible

16-20"Because of this decision we don't evaluate people by what they have or how they look. We looked at the Messiah that way once and got it all wrong, as you know. We certainly don't look at him that way anymore. Now we look inside, and what we see is that anyone united with the Messiah gets a fresh start, is created new. The old life is gone; a new life burgeons! Look at it! All this

comes from the God who settled the relationship between us and him, and then called us to settle our relationships with each other. God put the world square with himself through the Messiah, giving the world a fresh start by offering forgiveness of sins. God has given us the task of telling everyone what he is doing. We're Christ's representatives. God uses us to persuade men and women to drop their differences and enter into God's work of making things right between them. We're speaking for Christ himself now: Become friends with God; he's already a friend with you."

The good news about this passage is that our weaknesses, places of vulnerability, and areas of temptation can be changed. Jesus died to make us new! When you get in Christ and walk with Him, our old habits and vices start to pass away. We may be struggling with an area right now but we must understand that transformation is a process. When we go to school, we don't go from K-12 the same year. We go to Kindergarten and if we pass Kindergarten you go to 1st grade. 2 Corinthians 3:18 says that we go from glory to glory. Some of us are working too hard because we are trying to do too much at one time. We must let God take us one step at a time. Stop judging each other because some people have further to come from than others and more to deal with than others.

My father was a man who worked hard and loved his family; we didn't want for anything. But that's my story. If you are coming from a different background and your home life was chaotic, you didn't know who daddy was and mommy wouldn't tell you, your journey to wholeness and your doors will be different from mine. If you had all of that dysfunction it is going to take God a moment to bring some order to your life. Don't walk around with your head down feeling bad about it, but thank God that you have a chance to get it fixed. You don't have to walk around with your head down, because no one is better than you. None of us can knock each other because we all have some doors in need of repair. We all have some stuff that we need to work through, but thanks be to God that **if any man *be* in Christ, *he is* a new creature: old things are passed away; behold, all things are become new!**

I thought that when I got saved that transformation was an automatic thing. I said, "I have been up to the altar and received Jesus. I really love Him. Now, just fix me. Go on God, fix me." He said, "Not without your consent." I said, "No problem. Let's start praying about what needs to be fixed." I thought I was ready to handle it until God started to show me myself. What a humbling moment! Have you ever had God show you, you? I wasn't ready. I didn't have on my big girl dress. I thought that I was much better than I was, but when I began to look at myself through the lens of the Word of God I begin to see how far off I was. God began to show me, me and it hurt at first.

Truth has two components to it. Truth always hurts first, but if we hang in there and embrace it, it also heals. Most people get offended at the first stage of truth and they never get to the healing. The first person that was ever really honest with us and told us about ourselves, probably made us mad. People say that they want honesty and truth. People say, "I want a good pastor. I am tired of those crooked pastors." We get them all the time. They join our church and say, "I just love Pastor Karen." But the first time they sit in my office, we talk one-on-one, and I have to be honest, then it is over. They feel led to join somewhere else because their season is up. Some of us can't handle real friendships. Real friends will zero in and tell us exactly what we need to hear, because they really care about us.

If any man *be* in Christ, *he is* a new creature, only the process is not automatic. It is a journey that we have to enter into with our consent. When I was growing up I would look up to people and think that they were all just wonderful and beautiful. When I got saved and gave my life to the Lord I got the Holy Ghost for real. I started walking the walk and talking the talk. I found God's word to be so important in my life. I began to look around and observe the church world. I thought to myself, "Why are so many people in church not changing?" Have you noticed that all of us go to church together but everybody is not walking the same walk? Do you ever run into people from your church down at the market and they try to act like they don't see you? Are we suffering from an identity crisis? Are we spiritually schizophrenic? It began to baffle me.

I said, "God I don't understand, how can people be one way at church, pleasant when pastor is around, but then they don't speak to me at the gas station?" The Lord began to show me that the process of old things passing away requires the consent of the believer. Getting saved required our consent. Growing requires our consent also. When God starts to chisel away at us it is for the big girls and big boys, because not everyone is going to endure this process. When God starts to show us ourselves, we will have to part with some stuff. I am not talking about stuff that we are glad to see go, but we are going to have to let go of some things that we like. We are going to have to let go of some stuff that brings us attention and gets us a check every month. We are going to have to part with some things that we are married to. We have been doing them so long that we feel like we all are one. We are also going to have to part with some people or our new lifestyle will drive some people away.

Old things become new as we allow the Lord to make them new. We can't be envious of people who are reaping the rewards of obedience. They are paying the price. The choice to pay that same price and receive those blessings is ours also. Both of us are getting the harvest of our choice. We have to choose to let God work on us, and change things in us. When God comes after something from us, He has a replacement already lined up. If we don't give Him what He is asking for, then we don't get the replacement. When God came after my depression, He had joy in His other hand. I was so used to being sad before I got saved that I didn't feel normal if I wasn't sad or upset about something. It became my norm. I finally allowed God to shut that door for good.

When He began to come for that stuff, I held on for a minute, because it was like, "I don't feel right unless I'm sad. Leave me alone. I'm used to this. It's not good for me but I'm used to it. It's not working for me, but I'm comfortable with it. It is not right, but this is the way that I've been all of my life." When He finally got me to a place where I wasn't depressed every half a second, He began to pour in joy. I was like, "What's this? This feels good. This is calming me." I could be home alone and like my company. The peace that He put in me lasted when troubles came. It was different from anything I had experienced before. My new normal was being happy and peaceful. I have a new normal because old things were passing away and all things were becoming new. It was now normal for me to be happy. Misery is not the only one that loves company. Happy people love company! Fulfilled people love company! People who are full of joy and happiness want to share that.

If any man *be* in Christ, *he is* a new creature: old things are passed away. That means that whatever doors we were born with through our lineage, doors we gained through life experiences, and doors that we have gained due to ignorance are all passing away and we are in the process of becoming new. There are so many passages that confirm this promise. **Philippians 2:12, Wherefore, my beloved, as ye have always obeyed, not as in my presence only, but now much more in my absence, work out your own salvation with fear and trembling.** Work! If we are going to be transformed by the power of God, there is a part that God is going to do and a part that we are going to have to do. Many of us call ourselves waiting on God when in reality God is waiting on us. He is waiting on us to use what He has put in place. The process was completed at Calvary and now we have to consent to let it begin in our everyday lives.

In the natural we have to exercise our physical body in order to be healthy. In the spiritual realm we have to work out our salvation. It will only work if we work it. If I don't plug up the vacuum cleaner, I have a vacuum cleaner but my carpet will still stay a mess. It will only work if I work it. Some of that exercise equipment that you have in the closet will only work if you get on it. You are saying, "I have the thigh trimmer," but you are never on it so it's not helping your thighs. They are still touching, rubbing, and clapping every time you walk, because you are not working it out. Some of us get saved and we stop right there saying, "I'm saved, that's it." After salvation the journey to wholeness has to begin in order for us to become a new creature. We have to take our eyes off of everybody else that may be working theirs out, and mind our business. That is especially good for husbands and wives, because we are great observers. Some of us are excellent at noticing the cracks in other people's doors, when we have a great big hole in our door. Some of us notice that other people's doors need a paint job, when we don't have a knob anymore. We must work out our own salvation!

When I taught in Baltimore County Public schools we had a form in special education called an IEP. That stood for Individualized Educational Program. An IEP was an assessment of a student's strengths and weaknesses. We would look at the strengths of the student and then look and see what they were struggling with that was causing them not be on grade level with their peers. We would then write strategies to decrease or do away with their specific weak areas academically. The point of special education was not to label somebody, because nobody is dumb, except the devil. There is nobody dumber than someone who was in heaven and got put out. Those strategies on the IEP were written and implemented in order to address the weakness of that particular student. We need to be on an ISP, Individual Spiritual Plan. When we take an honest look at what our weaknesses are we will say, "God give me scriptures to treat this stuff."

When God began to deal with me I had a terrible temper. I thank God that He gives wisdom to the simple, because that is what I needed. God began to take me through the Word and show me scriptures on anger. By the time I started reading those scriptures on anger it didn't feel good to have an attitude and a temper anymore. The scripture that healed me was **Ecclesiastes 7:9b**, **"…for anger resteth in the bosom of fools."** How can you read that and still like being angry? I was so glad that I was alone when I read it because it cut me immediately. It hurt me first and then it began to heal me. It began to make me take a step back and instead of getting upset all of the time, take a deep breath and say, "God, I don't know what to do here. I am used to getting angry and doing something not beneficial. Show me what to do in these instances. Show me how to handle it." I began to let the Word treat me, and as the Word treated me old things began to pass away and all things began to get new.

If we are serious believers and serious about growth, we will be interested in bible study and consistent church attendance. We will want as much new information as we can get, so that we can treat our doors and keep them shut. Otherwise the devil will continue to trip us up in those areas that are open, naked, and vulnerable. Those of us who are working on something are trying to get all of the Word we can get. The Word is what changes us. The Word is what makes our process easier. The Word is what moves us along from glory to glory. The Word is what causes us to pass the trials, tribulations, tests, and exams. Once God teaches us, there will be a quiz and exam. The cares and trials of life are going to test us to see if we got it. It feels so good when we go through something that we have been through before but we handle it differently. It is a wonderful feeling when we can see ourselves growing and changing. No we are not perfect, but we are not what we used to be. In a minute we are not even going to look like this. It is encouraging. **If any man *be* in Christ he is a new creature!** Anybody that is in God for real doesn't have to stay the same unless they want to. It is a choice. God is so awesome and good that He wants it more for us than we want it for ourselves.

The transformation process won't happen automatically and it will take some work on our part. We must work out our own salvation with fear and trembling. Fear means reverence and respect for God. When God pulls us, we mustn't dare sit there and argue with Him. If God says we have to get it together, we have to get it together. We must humble ourselves and do what He says. He has our best interest in mind.

When God began to show me myself, there were some things that I didn't know were in me. When He showed me I didn't like it, it didn't feel good. God is God. How could I argue with God? I know truth hurts, but if we hold on to it, truth will heal us. We can't repair what we don't admit is broken. Only if we receive the truth will it make us free. It is the truth that we embrace. It is the truth that we receive. It is the truth that we allow in our lives that makes us free. We can go to a place called denial and act like it is not there, but that will stunt our development in the long run.

Work out your own salvation with fear and trembling. Be humble. When we talk about trembling we are talking about being in a place of humility. We are not talking about going around petrified. We cannot have a healthy relationship with somebody if we are scared to death. When God talks about fearing Him, He means reverential awe and honor. It means, don't deal with Him like He is on our level. It means respect Him for the place of holiness and sanctity that He holds. Respect and acknowledge His sovereignty. Trembling means honesty and humility. Trembling does not mean walking around putting ourselves down. Humility does not mean walking around unable to take a compliment, that's phony. *"Girl, that's a nice dress." "It ain't nothing." "Why did you buy it? Why did you pick that one off the rack and purchase it? It is nice and you know it is."* If somebody gives you a compliment say, "Thank you." You know that it is nice or you wouldn't have put it on.

Humility means to have an accurate understanding of both our strengths and weaknesses. Humble people are so in tune with themselves that they know where they are strong, and they also keep it real about where they are weak. That's why the devil can't fool them and trip them up because they know the areas in their life that if the enemy comes that way they will need prayer. Some of us are so phony that we don't know what our spots are. We don't know where our doors are. Every time the enemy comes he comes right through that same door. Have you noticed that you go through the same trial over and over again? Have you noticed that the enemy keeps getting you the same way because you have not acknowledged that door? You can't close a door that you won't acknowledge. You have to acknowledge it so that you can shut it.

Humble people keep it real. They are honest. They say, "God I am strong here, but I need help there. These things are naturally in my personality to be strong at, but these things are not. If you ask me to do something over in this area I am going to fumble it, need your help, and mess it up." People who are honest get delivered. People who are honest grow. I am so happy now that it is really hard to make me mad. I used to be mad all of the time, but now I am so happy that you have to really do something crazy and I mean really outlandish to upset me. I am so full of joy now. Joy is my new normal because old things have passed away in that particular area and that area is new. There are some other areas that I am still working on, because I am on a spiritual journey that is still taking me from glory to glory.

Some things about us God is not going to deal with us on yet because we can't take it. It is not His style to tear down, discourage, and hurt anybody. When God really deals with us in those private areas, most of the time it is just Him and us. If He has to always do it in the sanctuary it is because we are not spending enough honest time with Him at home. If He has to ALWAYS use other people to get our attention or our pastor has to ALWAYS address it in a message, He is not getting enough time with us.

Work out your own salvation. *"Why do we have to come to church? Can I just stay home and serve God. I don't have to be a part of a church. I don't even like church. Some of the preachers are crazy."* You are right. God still requires us to belong to a local household of faith because every time we come to church, God gives us more Word to help us work it out. Every song, every sermon, every dance, every poem is pouring more strength in us to help us work it out. Some places of our working are easy.

I used to smoke, and when I got saved two things happened. First, Pastor Linwood said he wasn't marrying anybody with cigarette breath. That was encouraging and kind of helped. The second thing was that I wanted to stop. We have areas where we want to stop and God says, "I'll give you the grace for that." There are other areas that are more challenging. Those are areas where we are comfortable. Those things that we still like and have a taste for require more work, more Word, and more support. Your local church has all of the above. We cannot repair those doors alone, but provision has been made for us to become a new creature. All our old things can pass away with our consent and effort by the grace of God.

"I am crucified with Christ: nevertheless I live; yet not I, but Christ liveth in me: and the life which I now live in the flesh I live by the faith of the Son of God, who loved me, and gave himself for me."

Galatians 2:20

Chapter Six: Jesus: THE Door Fixer!

"For as many as are led by the Spirit of God, they are the sons of God. 15 For ye have not received the spirit of bondage again to fear; but ye have received the Spirit of adoption, whereby we cry, Abba, Father. 16 The Spirit itself beareth witness with our spirit, that we are the children of God. "

Romans 8:14-16

Coming into the knowledge of one's vulnerabilities can be frightening, but there is good news! Jesus is THE ultimate door repairman! God will never show us our faults without letting us also know that He is and has the solution and cure for our situation. God never leaves us on a cliffhanger. He never calls us out and says, "This is not correct in you. This needs to be fixed" without saying, "I have the solution and the power." I am so thankful and excited today, that because of the shed blood of Jesus Christ we can have new life in the Lord.

When we come to the Lord, three things happen that cause us to be able to get our doors fixed! When we come to the Lord we gain a new position, new paternity, and new power!

We are born into the world in a corrupt state. That's not our fault. Adam made a choice and we all were born into it. That is why we don't have to teach children what's wrong to do; we have to teach them what is right to do. We come here knowing what's wrong to do and we can do it well, because it is in us. We can do it without thinking. A child will eat a cookie out of a jar that you asked them not to touch until after dinner and have crumbs all over his face. You will say, "Did you eat the cookie?" He will lie and answer, "No, I didn't eat the cookie." Lying at age two! Why? It is in us. I know that God has saved us, cleansed us, and we look beautiful now, but if God would ever take His grace off of us, can you imagine what we would look like down on the inside? You don't want to deal with the BC person: before Christ, before Calvary, before conversion. We all have a BC person waiting to get back in the driver's seat of our lives.

As born again believers in Christ, the good news about all of our issues is that, in Christ we have a new position. We have been made free! Some of us are out of jail, but are still walking around acting like we are in bondage. We are out of jail but we are still living behind bars of fear and failure. We can go from a victim to a victor! From being bound to being free! From being underneath our troubles to being on top of them!

Whatever doors we were born with through our lineage, whatever doors we gained though life's experiences, and whatever doors we may have due to ignorance, are all passing away because we are in the process of becoming new. Some of us are caught up in the fact that everything about us is not quite lovely yet. Don't get caught up there, because it is the trick of the enemy to focus us on what we used to be. If we take a good look at our godly self right now, we are not even close to what we were when God got His hands on us. Some of us didn't know that we could be happy, and now we are full of joy. Some of us didn't know that we could be victorious, and now we are victorious on a regular basis. Some of us didn't know that the devil existed and now we not only know that he exists, but we also know how to defeat him, rebuke him, and put him under our feet! Some of us didn't know that our flesh was so weak, but now we are on top of that, because what used to tempt us doesn't stand a chance now. The doors that used to be open, now many of them are shut. Keep growing and keep closing those doors!

In Ephesians 2:4-6 there are some powerful truths about our new location. We need to understand that we have a new position, a new location. Very few people who have lived in a crammed apartment for a long time, and get blessed with a house, ever want to return to the apartment. Some of us remember when we didn't have it like we have it right now. Some of us remember when there wasn't enough space to change our clothes in our bedroom and now look at what God has done. For those of us that are not too ashamed or humble to remember, I dare say that after God brought us out of some of those areas of our lives and seasons that we are not dying to get back to them.

Ephesians 2:1-6, AND YOU *hath he quickened,* who were dead in trespasses and sins; Wherein in time past ye walked according to the course of this world, according to the prince of the power of the air, the spirit that now worketh in the children of disobedience. Among whom also we all had our conversation in times past in the lusts of our flesh, fulfilling the desires of the flesh and of the mind; and were by nature the children of wrath, even as others. Conversation in this text means behavior. Many of us, at some point, acted like the folks on the Jerry Springer show. Even if we hid it, we had it down in us. If God would release some of us, we could go right back there and remember how to do it. We know how to pop our neck. It is in us; we are just not walking in it now because we are standing on top of it. We are on top of what used to be on top of us. We now have what used to have us. Our position has changed!

But God, who is rich in mercy, for his great love wherewith he loved us. Even when we were dead in sins, hath quickened us together with Christ, (by grace ye are saved;) And hath raised us up together, and made us sit together in heavenly *places* in Christ Jesus. Some things are hard to understand because they are not tangible or literal. We have to conceptualize it in our mind. It is not a physical thing, but a reality in the realm of the spirit. When it says that we have been raised up together, it does not mean physically that we live in the galaxy. We are no longer conformed to this world system. (Romans 12:1-2) We do not operate according to this system. Even though we are *in* the world, we are not *of* the world. Now that we are saved we have been shifted above what used to be on top of us. The challenges that used to hem us up and cause us to fail do not have the same effect on us now. When we got delivered and began to shut those open doors, God gave us the power to take that thing and toss it. Now instead of it being on top of us, we are on top of it! We now have a choice whether or not we sin. Now when weaknesses try to rise up in our flesh, we take authority over them. I have a habit of saying, "I am not going to walk in that." What I am really saying is, "I'm feeling a temptation." I am in tune with the fact that there is a temptation going on right now and a struggle in my members. They are trying to decide who is going to win and they are waiting for the confession out of my mouth to see what side is going to have its way.

Now I have the grace of God, the power of God, and resources from the Holy Ghost that I don't possess in the natural. Instead of acting like I used to, I now have a choice whether I am going to glorify God or get in my flesh. That being said, everything is not the devil. Some things are those doors. Some things are my choice. If we have been given a new position, we are now seated together in heavenly places in Christ, meaning we have dominion. We are reigning. When we reign, we are over something. What are we reigning over? Sin? Sickness? Depression? Suicide? Negative attitudes? Selfishness?

With this new position we don't have to act like we did in our old position. We know what it means to get promoted. We have been promoted from shame and sin to victory and power! **Colossians 1:21, And you, that were sometime alienated and enemies in**

***your* mind by wicked works, yet now hath he reconciled.** Reconciled means to become compatible or consistent; to reestablish a close relationship with; to settle or resolve. Many people who work for the bank will tell you that at the end of their shift they have to reconcile their drawer. Everything has to add up on paper and in the drawer. God reconciled us, because the life that He meant for us to have is not the one that we came into the earth living. He came to reconcile us to make sure that our life adds up to what He has on paper. We were born to be victorious. We were born to be more than a conqueror. When He comes to reconcile us He wants to make sure that His promises are activated in our life. He doesn't want them just written in the Bible, but He wants them operating in our life from Sunday to Saturday!

God wants to make sure that blessings of Deuteronomy chapter 28 overtake us. To do that, there has to be a positional change. There has to be a new direction. Our ways have to begin to line up with His ways. **Amos 3:3, Can two walk together, except they be agreed?** Ask any married couple and they will tell you that their unity is not a magic. Some choices have been made. There is a common bond. When you see any type of relationship, the people in it have something in common. What makes you draw to one person over another is that the two of you have something in common. What makes us draw nearer to His precious bleeding side is that we are now the redeemed of the Lord! We have been reconciled. We have been brought back to His bosom. We have been placed back with our daddy. He wants to give us the abundant life that He originally planned for us! (John 10:10)

We also have a new paternity. Before I got saved I was very religious. I thought I knew a lot about God and every now and then I would misquote a scripture or two. The truth is, I didn't know the Old Testament from the New Testament. I used to walk around saying things like, "We are all God's children." Until I read John 8:44. **"Ye are of *your* father the devil, and the lusts of your father ye will do. He was a murderer from the beginning, and abode not in the truth, because there is no truth in him. When he speaketh a lie, he speaketh of his own: for he is a liar, and the father of it."**

Jesus told them, "You are not from my daddy but you are of your daddy the devil." How do you know who your father is? By your bloodline! A child's paternity is not determined by the mother's blood, but by the father's bloodline. For those of us who declared that we are blessed, highly favored, let us check out our fruit and we will tell you which bloodline we are activating and living out of for real. Faith confessions without works are dead and just words. The bloodline that we all have coming into this life is of the devil. Adam made a choice that set all of us off and that was not our fault. It we let things remain that way then the accountability rests with us. If you want to change it, help is available.

As new believers, we have a new position, and our paternity changes. It is not going to change automatically. Jesus died for everybody, but we have to accept what He purchased for us personally and individually. If you have a washing machine, but don't use it, your clothes will still stay dirty. There is A Savior, but He has to become OUR Savior. All of us have toothbrushes, but all of us don't use them. I decree and declare that some folks never heard of Listerine. I am trying to get you to understand that just because something is available doesn't mean that we are taking advantage of it. It doesn't mean that we have used it. Yes, Jesus died for the world, but the entire world hasn't cashed in on it and everyone does not choose to be reconciled. When we give our life to Christ, we get a new paternity and a new daddy.

The bloodline of one Father cancels out the bloodline of the other! Thank you Jesus! **Romans 8:14-16, For as many as are led by the Spirit of God, they are the sons of God. For ye have not**

received the spirit of bondage again to fear; but ye have received the Spirit of adoption, whereby we cry, Abba, Father. The Spirit itself beareth witness with our spirit, that we are the children of God.

Now we are no longer a child of the enemy, because our life is righteous, and we have fruit unto repentance, fruit of the Spirit, love, joy, peace, longsuffering, temperance, goodness, faith, meekness, and temperance. Now we can look at our fruit and we can tell who our daddy is because you have a new paternity. Every door that we receive through our lineage can be canceled out through our new lineage. The blood of our new daddy can wipe out the faults of our old daddy. Now it doesn't matter if our daddy was an alcoholic, because our new bloodline will put a different taste in our mouth and replace the cravings for alcohol. It doesn't matter if our old daddy was a wife-abuser; we don't have to walk in that, because our new daddy said, "Love your wife as Christ loves the church." Our new daddy has different operating rules. Our new daddy's blood is more potent and powerful. He has never lost His power, so you need to just make up in our mind that we are going to give Him His blood's worth out of our life. I am not going to play with our blood. I am not going to waste our blood. I am going to ***walk*** in the power, ***talk*** in the power, ***live*** in the power,

think in the power, ***make decisions*** in the power, ***obey Him*** through the power, ***live right*** by the power, and ***walk in His Word*** by the power.

Sickness was in our old bloodline, but healing is in this one. Negativity was in our old bloodline, but word confession is in our new one. Fear was in our old bloodline, but boldness and power is in our new daddy's bloodline. That is encouraging, because some of us may not talk about it much, but some of us came from some pretty messed up families. Growing up I thought that I was the only person with a dysfunctional family until I got old enough to realize that most of the people on my block were going through too. No one talked about it. The grass looked greener but it still had to be mowed. We don't have to be ashamed because of what's behind door #2. I promise you that my door #3 will blow your door #2 away. We have some stuff in the closet that we don't want to talk about. When you get a new paternity and a new bloodline, we will go from dysfunction to function, from chaos to order, from drama to blessings!

We shouldn't walk around letting people put us down because of where we come from, who we come from, where we've been, and how we were raised. We must not let anybody tell us that we are nobody, because, "**If any man be in Christ he is a new creature, old things are passed away**." Sometimes the reason people may talk about our past because our future is so awesome that they can't find anything right now to point out about us. They say, "Let me go back ten years." If somebody has to go back that far to criticize us, that is an indication that there is not much there to pick at now! We have been victorious for so long that they don't have anything recent to mess with us about.

Sometimes people will want to put their mouth on us while God is working on us. It indicts them, because they have limited vision. Any fool can see what's happening in the present, but it takes somebody that is connected to God to look at what is a mess and know that it will end up being a message. If we were to look at a jacked up life right now, we would hear God say, "I am going to put all of those pieces in place. Don't you worry about it, I am going to work you like a puzzle. It might not be right now, but I am going to shift everything until it fits where it is supposed to fit, until that puzzle picture looks like the image that I created of you from the beginning of time. Don't worry about your puzzle pieces right now because I have the power to put all of them in their proper places. Don't worry about the people that have your picture mixed up right now because they can't see what I see."

Last but not least, we have been given new power! **Roman 8:10-12, And if Christ *be* in you, the body *is* dead because of sin; but the Spirit *is* life because of righteousness. But if the Spirit of him that raised up Jesus from the dead dwell in you, he that raised up Christ from the dead shall also quicken your mortal bodies by his Spirit that dwelleth in you. Therefore, brethren, we are debtors, not to the flesh, to live after the flesh.**

How many people have ever shopped and purchased a generic brand? It is supposed to do the same thing as a name brand, but it's generic. I always tell people, when you come to my house for a cookout, "Don't bring Cola Pop." Don't bring those three for five-dollar deals, because they are full of sugar and they are not healthy. It is not that I am being arrogant or can't drink that, but I have enough knowledge now to know that some things we don't need to put in our body. That is why it is on sale, they are trying to get rid of it. It doesn't cost that much, because it's not valuable. What is good for us sometimes costs a lot.

When we read in the passage, **if the Spirit of him that raised up Jesus from the dead dwell in you,** we learn that God didn't give us a generic brand or a diluted Holy Ghost. He didn't give us something left over after He finished everything else that He was doing. He has given us the same power that raised Jesus from the dead! We don't have a little portion or generic brand of Holy Ghost; we have the authentic power of God working in our life. If that same power that dwells in us was able to get a dead man out of a tomb, imagine what it does to our doors! It also resurrects every dead thing in us that needs to come back to life!

Remember the dreams and aspirations we had as children? Every good thing that God put in us that sin has tainted, the resurrecting power of Jesus has now come to revive! The old things are passing away and all things are becoming new. When the power reconciles us it gets in us and starts to resurrect our dreams, passion, plans, destiny, future, and vision that God gave us as children. As a child, we saw ourselves doing well in life. Are we? As a child, we saw certain things for our future. Are we there? When the power of the Holy Ghost comes upon us, we receive the same power that got Jesus out of a tomb, the same power that got Him out of a place where people said, "He's done. It's over. We watched him die." The same people that used to sit around saying that we were washed up and done are now going to see us rise! Where they thought we were when they left off they will have to deal with the new us that got up in power, got up in purpose, got up in vision, got up victorious, and got up a winner!

God did not give a generic, knock off or 'wanna be' spirit to us, but He sent the same power into us that He gave Jesus to get out of the tomb. **Colossians 2:10, And ye are complete in him, which is the head of all principality and power.** All we have to do is recognize that we are in a new position and start walking it out. We are in the position that He predestined for us to be in before the world began! It is my reality. It is where I live at. We now live a "can't lose" life. I live in the zone of impossibility because I have the same power that raised Jesus, and it is raising me to new levels of knowledge and victory everyday.

As believers, we have been given new position, new paternity, and new power! We can shut every door no matter how it became opened in the first place and no matter how long is has been there. If ANY man is in Christ he can become new!

Make Jesus YOUR Savior Today!

Pray this prayer sincerely from your heart:

"Lord I come to you today realizing my need for you. I believe in my heart that Jesus died for my sins and was raised from the dead in order to give me eternal life. I realize that I have doors in my life that no one can heal but you. I come to you now asking you to be MY Savior. Come into my heart and cleanse me, change me, and give me the power to grow. I know that I can expect to walk in newness of life as I learn and study your Word. Please point me in the direction of a Bible believing and teaching church so that I may grow in you and become the person you designed me to be. Thank you for saving me. In Jesus' name I pray. Amen."

If you prayed this prayer please contact us at 410-265-6800 for a free book to help you begin to grow and mature.